WHITE HOUSE INSIDERS

What's It Like to
WORK IN THE WHITE HOUSE?

BY KATHLEEN CONNORS

Gareth Stevens
PUBLISHING

Please visit our website, www.garethstevens.com. For a free color catalog of all our high-quality books, call toll free 1-800-542-2595 or fax 1-877-542-2596.

Library of Congress Cataloging-in-Publication Data

Connors, Kathleen.
What's it like to work in the White House? / by Kathleen Connors.
p. cm. — (White House insiders)
Includes index.
ISBN 978-1-4824-1116-4 (pbk.)
ISBN 978-1-4824-1117-1 (6-pack)
ISBN 978-1-4824-1115-7 (library binding)
1. White House (Washington, D.C.) — Juvenile literature. 2. Washington (D.C.) — Buildings, structures, etc. — Juvenile literature. 3. White House (Washington, D.C.) — Miscellanea — Juvenile literature. I. Connors, Kathleen. II. Title.
F204.W5 C66 2015
975.3—d23

First Edition

Published in 2015 by
Gareth Stevens Publishing
111 East 14th Street, Suite 349
New York, NY 10003

Copyright © 2015 Gareth Stevens Publishing

Designer: Nick Domiano
Editor: Kristen Rajczak

Photo credits: Cover, pp. 1 (chef), 5, 15 Chip Somodevilla/Getty Images News/Getty Images; cover, p. 1 (Secret Service agent) 1000 Words/Shutterstock.com; cover, pp. 1, 13 (Angella Reid) Carolyn Kaster/AP Photos; p. 7 David Valdez/White House/Time Life Pictures/Getty Images; p. 9 Mandel Ngan/AFP/Getty Images; p. 11 Cg-realms/Wikimedia Commons; p. 17 Wilfredo Lee/AP Photos; p. 19 Mike Theiler/Getty Images News/Getty Images; p. 20 Tgprn Glamour/AP Photos.

Printed in the United States of America

CPSIA compliance information: Batch #CS15GS: For further information contact Gareth Stevens, New York, New York at 1-800-542-2595.

Contents

Words in the glossary appear in **bold** type the first time they are used in the text.

Super Staff

Those who work at the White House have many tasks, from gardening to speaking with the press. Some work behind the scenes, while others are more public. However, they have one thing in common: they all work for the president.

Former chief usher of the White House Stephen Rochon said, "There is no normal day in the White House. Every day is different." Whether a White House staff member works in the East Wing or the West Wing, that's something they can agree on!

The Inside Scoop

The White House's West Wing is where the president's **political** staff works. The Oval Office is there, too. The East Wing includes the First Family's **residence** and the State Floor where White House tours, state dinners, and events are held.

President Barack Obama wouldn't be able to have such organized press conferences without his staff helping to plan them.

The Executive Office
of the President

All the people, departments, and offices that support the president form the **Executive** Office of the President. Officially established by Congress in 1939, more than 1,700 people work in the many parts of the Executive Office. The White House Office is one part of the Executive Office of the President.

The White House Office is made up of the president's closest advisers, those who arrange his schedule, the Office of the First Lady, and more. Both West Wing and East Wing workers are included.

The Inside Scoop

Some of the White House staff, such as many of those in the residence, stay the same from **administration** to administration. Others, including the many advisers in the West Wing, change with every president.

The White House Office was first established as a group of people who would help the president with his day-to-day tasks in running the country. Here, President George H. W. Bush (fourth from right) speaks to advisers.

7

Chief of Staff

The president's chief of staff was once known as simply the assistant to the president. Today, the chief of staff is the top position in the West Wing. It's an honor to be named chief of staff—but it's a big job.

The chief of staff oversees the highest White House staffers, works with Congress and government departments, and often controls who speaks to the president. In general, the chief of staff works to further the president's **agenda**, such as gun control, education, or health care.

The Inside Scoop

Working in the West Wing can be **stressful**. To have fun and stay in shape, some staffers have said they play basketball together. There's also a White House softball team!

Chief of staff is such a tough job that the average term is only 2 1/2 years! Rahm Emanuel was President Obama's first chief of staff. Then, he left to become mayor of Chicago.

In the West Wing

The **deputy** chiefs of staff, speechwriters, and the president's senior advisers all work in the West Wing. But the West Wing is never just the president's staff. Members of Congress, the press, and foreign leaders often do business in the West Wing. That makes it a pretty busy place!

Working in the West Wing commonly means long hours, and the work doesn't end when staffers go home. Many are "on call"—or able to be called—at all times to deal with problems that come up.

The Inside Scoop

The president has many assistants, including a big group of presidential aides. Aides often want top political jobs someday, such as chief of staff. They work long hours and do thankless tasks to get there.

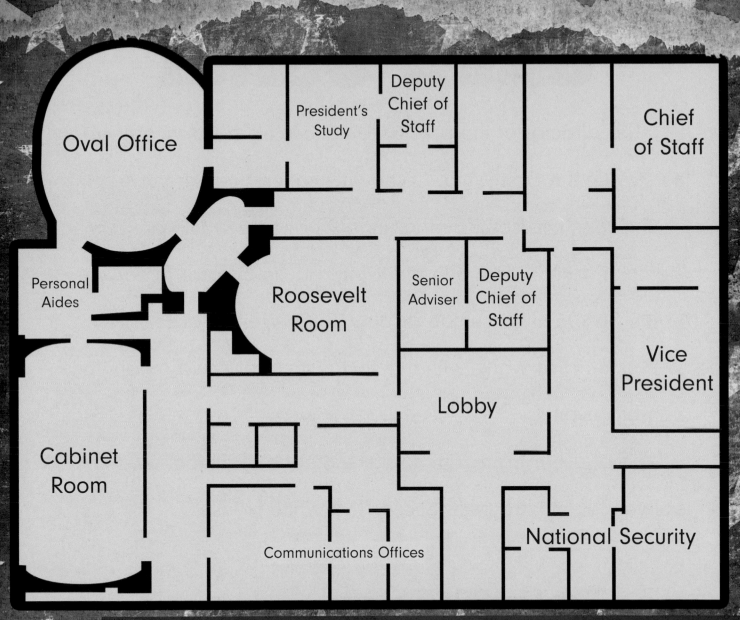

Oval Office

President's Study

Deputy Chief of Staff

Chief of Staff

Personal Aides

Roosevelt Room

Senior Adviser

Deputy Chief of Staff

Vice President

Lobby

Cabinet Room

National Security

Communications Offices

This picture shows the layout of the first floor of the West Wing during President Barack Obama's presidency. Notice the **Cabinet** Room near the Oval Office. That's where the president meets with the heads of government departments, such as defense.

Chief Usher

The director of the president's executive residence heads the staff in the East Wing. Commonly called the chief usher, this job includes overseeing more than 90 people who work there. The chief usher works with the White House **curator** in caring for the historical pieces on display in the White House. The chief usher also works with the social secretary and others to plan big events.

Chief usher from 2007 to 2011, Stephen Rochon, said his job was "to put the best face on the White House."

The Inside Scoop

When the Obama family moved into the White House in 2009, it only took a few hours to move President Bush and First Lady Laura Bush out and the new First Family in. This was thanks to the organization of the chief usher and the residence staff!

Angella Reid became the first woman to be chief usher in 2011. She's only the ninth person ever to hold the job!

13

Residence Staff

Those who work in the East Wing are in charge of the White House residence and the State Floor. An executive housekeeper heads a staff that dusts, vacuums, and mops their way to a spotless place for tourists and the First Family to enjoy.

Butlers are central to the daily activities of the East Wing, too. They may get the newspaper for the president in the morning, set up for a state dinner in the afternoon, and serve tea to a foreign leader in the evening.

The Inside Scoop

The staff in the residence have to start work in the early morning to be ready for the First Family to start their day. Because of this, they often only work until the midafternoon, unless there's an event at night.

First Lady Laura Bush worked with the East Wing Staff to plan a state dinner honoring Queen Elizabeth II of England in 2007.

15

What's Cooking?

Whether the queen of England is visiting or the First Family is having dinner alone, the executive chef of the White House is planning the menu. White House executive chef Cris Comerford has said each has **challenges**, but doing both "makes you grow as a chef."

The executive pastry chef makes the fancy desserts served at parties and dinners. They're often very **detailed**, such as cookies with pictures of the White House on them. The White House even has its own chocolate shop where treats are made!

The Inside Scoop

One of the executive pastry chef's jobs during the year is the White House gingerbread house. In 1993, the gingerbread house built for President Bill Clinton's first Christmas at the White House took 200 hours to make!

This picture shows First Lady Hillary Clinton and White House pastry chefs presenting the yearly gingerbread house in 1997.

17

Guarding the Grounds

Protecting the president, the First Family, and those working in the high-profile White House is an important and sometimes dangerous job. In 1922, the White House Police Force was established. It became part of the Secret Service in 1930.

In 2010, there were about 1,300 members of the Secret Service Uniformed Division, or the part of the Secret Service that protects the White House, the vice president's residence, and the US Treasury. They carefully patrol the White House grounds, ready to spring into action when needed.

The Inside Scoop

The Secret Service is the group that protects the president and First Family, members of Congress, and other important people in the government. They also protect foreign leaders when they're in the country.

The Secret Service Uniformed Division can make those who work at the White House feel safe.

Job Openings

Would you like to work at the White House? No matter what kind of job you want, there will be a background check. The Federal Bureau of Investigation (FBI) might even visit your friends and family and call other places you've worked.

One way to start a career at the White House is through an internship. White House interns aren't paid but they learn job skills in one of the most famous workplaces in America!

White House Interns

The Inside Scoop

White House interns commonly need to be at least 18 years old and in college. Many use an internship at the White House for college credit.

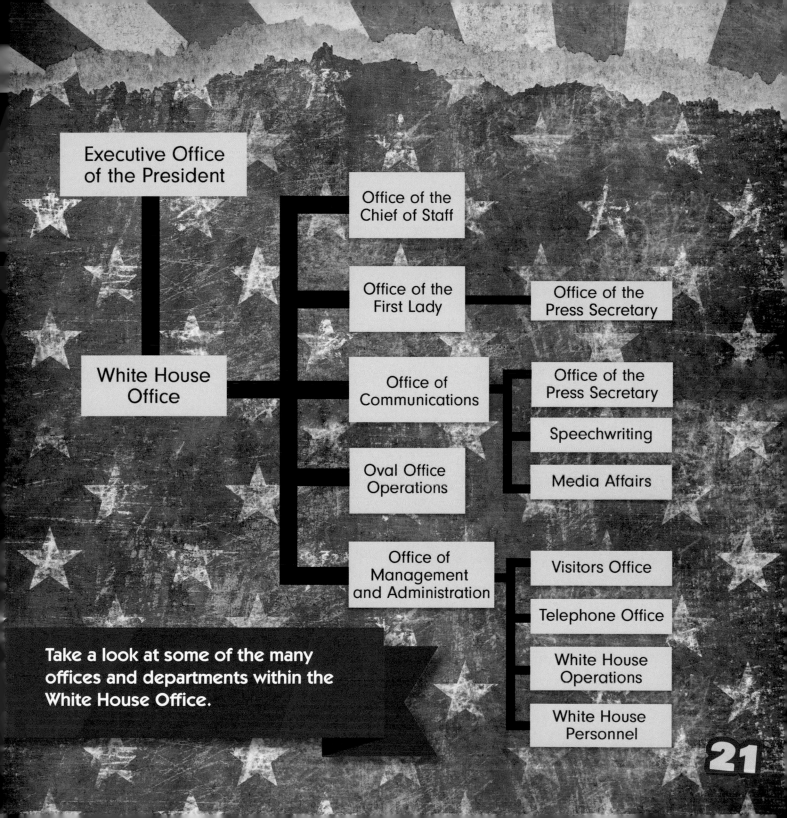

Executive Office of the President

White House Office

Office of the Chief of Staff

Office of the First Lady

Office of Communications

Oval Office Operations

Office of Management and Administration

Office of the Press Secretary

Office of the Press Secretary

Speechwriting

Media Affairs

Visitors Office

Telephone Office

White House Operations

White House Personnel

Take a look at some of the many offices and departments within the White House Office.

Glossary

administration: term of office

agenda: things someone wants to get done or talk about

Cabinet: the president's closest advisers who head the major government departments

challenge: a test of abilities

curator: a person whose job it is to care for something. Curators often work in museums or places with other kinds of exhibits.

deputy: assistant

detailed: including many small parts

executive: having to do with the carrying out of the law. Also, a person who manages or directs.

political: having to do with the activities of the government and government officials

protect: to keep safe

residence: home

stressful: full of stress, or a feeling of worry

For More Information

BOOKS

House, Katherine L. *The White House for Kids: A History of a Home, Office, and National Symbol with 21 Activities.* Chicago, IL: Chicago Review Press, 2014.

Kennedy, Marge. *Who Works at the White House?* New York, NY: Children's Press, 2009.

WEBSITES

The White House Kitchen
whitehouse.c-span.org/Video/WhiteHouseStaff/ WhiteHouse-Kitchen.aspx
Watch a video of the White House's kitchen staff preparing for a big dinner for the queen of England!

The Working White House
www.whitehousehistory.org/whha_exhibits/working_whitehouse/
Check out lots of information about working at the White House through the years, and see pictures of staff members.

Index